ENJOYING THE RECEIVING PROCESS

ENJOYING THE RECEIVING PROCESS

Dr. Richard D. Holmes, Sr.

XULON ELITE

Xulon Press Elite
2301 Lucien Way #415
Maitland, FL 32751
407.339.4217
www.xulonpress.com

Unless otherwise indicated, Scripture quotations taken from the King James Version (KJV)–*public domain.*

Scripture quotations taken from the Amplified Bible (AMP). Copyright © 1954, 1958, 1962, 1964, 1965, 1987 by The Lockman Foundation. Used by permission. All rights reserved.

Paperback ISBN-13: 978-1-66286-196-3
Ebook ISBN-13: 978-1-66286-197-0

DEDICATION AND THANKS

"O give thanks unto the Lord, for He is good: for His mercy endureth forever" (Psalms 107:1).

This book is dedicated to my wife, sweetheart, girlfriend, and partner in life, Dr Lydecia A. Holmes. It is because of her love, faithfulness, support, encouragement, and inspiration that I am able to pursue my calling and purpose with boldness and freedom.

To my sons, RaeDaeon, Richard D. Jr., DeAndre, and Richaun. Thanks for all of your patience and allowing me to be used of God. To my daughters-in-love, Shauta and Kassy. Thanks for all of your encouragement and allowing me to be in your lives.

To my spiritual parents, Apostle I V and Pastor Lady Bridget Hilliard. Thanks for all the teachings you have given to my wife and me. You are great examples in the body of Christ of real, genuine leadership and excellence.

To Morning View Word Church, "where you always get a fresh look at Jesus." Thanks for all your prayers and faithful support throughout the years. Love you much!

Dr. Richard D. Holmes Sr.

TABLE OF CONTENTS

FOREWORD

Dr. Richard Holmes steps out of the crowd to document his experiences in learning to live by faith. This most recent literary work is a unique teaching, testimony style presentation that will both inspire and instruct you in the practice of victorious living. This simple but solid approach to the message of faith is easy reading but is most effective in communicating this truth.

I love the Scripture based expository approach to this most interesting subject. Living by faith is not for the faint of heart and the disciplined resolve to apply the principles of faith over and over is what will ultimately yield the promised results of the Word of God. Dr. Holmes uses the testimonies of his real life victorious experiences to demonstrate how the revelation on the receiving process the Holy Spirit has given him is practiced.

The final chapter has transparent episodes from the lives of the Holmes family that will encourage all who may be facing similar setbacks. In reading "Enjoying The Receiving Process" you will be inspired to believe and receive the supernatural life Jesus came to give us. I am blessed to have Dr. Holmes as a spiritual son and can attest to his faithfulness to God, his family, his church and the kingdom of God. I have watched him use the principles of faith to overcome the various difficulties he has faced. You have in your hands a nugget of wisdom so value it as you read this revelation. Happy Reading!

Apostle I. V. Hilliard
New Light Christian Center Church, Founder

Association of Independent Ministry, Presiding Prelate
Hilliard International Ministries
Houston, Texas

Introduction

It is the will of God that every believer experience victory, success, and prosperity in every area of their lives. It is through the supernatural Word of God that we can tap into the abundant life that Jesus came to give. Scripture says, "The thief comes only in order to steal, kill and destroy. I came that they might have and enjoy life, and have it in abundance [to the fullest, till it overflows" (John 10:10 AMP). This is the order of God for our lives—abundant living!

I know God has made abundant living available for all believers, but I believe that in order to live in abundance, there must be purposeful effort in understanding that God has already provided everything we should ever need in life. Believers just need to learn how to navigate the process of receiving what is already theirs.

Many believers do not like the idea of entering into a **process**, but process is not a bad thing. When I write about "process," I am describing the continual forward movement from one point to another on the way to the completion of a goal. "Process" is a series of actions or steps taken in order to achieve a particular result. Please note … The opposite of process is disorder. Our God is a God of order!

The Spirit of God **led** me to write this book to give wisdom and insight from His Word, concerning this area of biblical receiving. Biblical receiving is about welcoming into your life those things which you believed from the Word of God. This process will be expanded upon in the first chapter. God has plans, purposes, and many promises for you, but there is a process you have to enter into to manifest those divine conditions in your life.

While reading and studying this book, remember that you are not to live your life as a believer only but also as a receiver. All the promises of God must be believed and then received by faith.

R-ecognize **E**-verything **C**-hrist **E**-stablished **I**-s **V**-ictory **E**-verlasting

Enjoy the receiving process.

Chapter 1

Understanding
Biblical Receiving

N ow that you are a believer and desire the best from God, it is crit-
ical that you understand biblical receiving and how to operate
in it. It is your responsibility to receive what God has promised you. It
is not your mother, father, sister, or brother's responsibility to receive
for you. It is *your* responsibility to receive. Thank God for the apostle,
prophet, evangelist, pastor, or teacher in your life ministering to you,
but when it comes down to the promises of God manifesting in your
life, *you* must do the receiving of those promises.

Please understand this: Faith is simply information from God that
He expects you to believe and act on. Receiving from God is the product
of you gathering information from God in His words and believing the
information to the point that you are acting on the information. Once
you act on the Word of God, you can shift to the mode of receiving.

Here is what took my wife and I to another level in ushering in
the promises of God in our lives—receiving a revelation on the word
"receive." The word **"RECEIVE"** may look passive, but it requires
action on your part.

The New Strong's Exhaustive Concordance Of The Bible defines
the greek word for "receive" (#2983) as *"lambano,"* which means to
grab hold of something. It means to take something, to catch something,

or accept something. In other words, you are actively involved in doing something.

> Mark 11:24 says, *"Therefore I say unto you, What things soever ye desire, when you pray, believe that ye receive them, and ye shall have them ..."*

> Galatians 3:14 says, *"That the blessing of Abraham might come on the Gentiles through Jesus Christ; that we might receive the promise Of the Spirit through faith."*

> 1 John 3:22 says, *"And whatever we ask we receive of Him because we keep His commandments, and do those things that are pleasing in His sight."*

> John 1:12 says, *"Have you received Jesus as your personal savior?"*

Have you actually done something to start receiving? I ask you this because receiving Jesus as your personal Savior requires action on your part.

Your mind must be renewed when it comes to receiving promises from our Heavenly Father. Receiving is not just sitting back, passively waiting on God to drop what we need in our lap while we just sit at home doing nothing!

I know God is a sovereign God, Who has all power and could place a million dollars in your mailbox today, but believe me, there is another way. I believe there is a predominate way you actively receive His promises by faith. The predominate way to receive is to make sure you are actively involved in doing the necessary and required action(s) to take hold of what you are believing.

Now that the meaning of "receive" has been defined, let me give you a definition of "biblical receiving." **Biblical receiving is simply** taking hold of and welcoming into your life that which you believe and act on from the Word of God.

Biblical receiving is not something that God provides automatically. We must first *do something* to receive the promises that God has already assured us. The reception, receiving, taking, catching, and welcoming of the promises of God is something we do as an act of faith. Recognize that the promises of God are yours because you are a believer. Go ahead and grab hold of them and welcome them into your life. Talk to the promises. Throw a reception party and let the promises know how welcome they are in your life.

Chapter 2

THE LAW OF RECEIVING

M any people ask the questions, "How do I change my life situation?" or "How do I fix what is wrong in my life?" or "How do I get the promises of God to manifest in my life?" Have you ever asked those questions?

Well, you begin answering those questions by understanding that God has set order in the earth. We must learn and respect His order and abide by His order to experience the results that we desire in our lives.

You have to be fully aware that there are laws governing everything in existence. You may ask, what then is a "law"? The Merriam-Webster Dictionary give a simple definition that a law is an established rule or principle that works the same way every time. A law is based on a predictable consequence of a certain act or action.

There are natural, physical laws that govern the natural, physical world. One such law is gravity. If the law of gravity was not operative, we would be floating all over planet earth.

Then there are God's spiritual laws that are higher and more powerful than the laws of nature and will supersede them every time. When a person learns to respect and cooperate with God's spiritual laws, that person will begin to experience victory, success, and prosperity in their lives.

One such spiritual law is receiving. **The law of receiving is simply depositing the words of God into your heart through the process of**

hearing, seeing, and speaking the words and sayings of God. Notice what the Bible says in Proverbs 4:20-21: "My son attend to my words; incline thine ear unto my sayings. Let them [words and sayings] not depart from thine eyes; keep them in the midst of thine heart."

In biblical Hebrew, the word "heart" describes where we feel feelings, think thoughts, and make choices. In biblical Greek, the word "heart" expresses the thoughts or feelings of the mind. So, in Scripture, the word "heart" is not referring to the hollow, muscular organ that expands and contracts to move blood through the arteries and veins. **Scripture uses the word "heart" to refer to all that is within us, namely, our human spirit and our soul**. For practical purposes, the heart means *our inner life*, which is the human spirit and soul. It is very important that you understand this because the law of receiving hinges on this information.

Notice again, in Proverbs 4 verse 20, Scripture tells us to pay attention to God's words. The enemy is fighting for your attention. Do not allow yourself to just sit around and listen to and watch the latest news of doom and disaster or the latest movies, but it's highly important that you pay attention to God's words. How does a person pay attention to God's words? First of all, by *hearing* God's words. Scripture says, "Incline thine ear." If need be, pull on your ear to make sure you are hearing His words. This is the very first way to pay attention—**by hearing God's words.** You should listen to the word of God daily by watching word based programming, via online, books and speaking the Word of God out loud.

Then, notice that verse 21 says, "let them not depart from thine eyes." What is "them"? "Them" refers to the words and sayings of God. So, the second way you pay attention is by *consistently looking into the words of God.* You actively read the words of God and allow them to go through your eyes. Let your ears hear and your eyes see what God is saying in His word.

The third way to pay attention to God's words is by keeping His words and sayings in the midst of your heart. Why should you keep the words of God in the midst of your heart? Proverbs 4 verse 22 says "For they are life unto those that find them, and health to all their flesh". We should keep the words and saying of God because they are life and health to those that find them.

In Proverbs chapter 4 verse 23, I want you to notice the word "keep." According to The New Strong's Exhaustive Concordance Of The Bible, the word "keep" means to put a hedge around. "Keep" also means to hem in, enclose, or bound. Another definition that I really like is "to protect and guard." So, here is what the scripture is saying when it comes down to the words of God and you: It is your responsibility to hem in, enclose, protect, and guard the words of God that are in the midst of your heart.

Now, why is it that we need to do all of these things? Look at Proverbs 4 verse 23: "Keep thy heart with all diligence; for out of it are the issues of life." The Amplified Bible says, "Keep and guard your heart with all vigilance and above all that you guard, for out of it FLOW THE SPRING OF LIFE" (emphasis added). This means that every-thing you do in life flows from your heart. **GUARD AND PROTECT YOUR HEART!**

I believe the verses we just studied are all saying, "TAKE WHAT GOD SAYS SERIOUSLY!"

The question has been asked, how does a person allow the words of God, that are full of God's faith and power, into their heart? The answer is, a person allows the words of God, that are full of God's faith and power, into their hearts through their eyes, ears, and mouth. The eyes, ears, and mouth are the three entrances into the heart of man.

Remember, the scripture says in Proverbs Chapter 4:20-21 "Incline thine ear **[your ears]** to my sayings." The scripture continues to say, "Let them sayings not depart from thine eyes **[your eyes]**." Matthew 12:34b says, "for out of the abundance of the heart, the mouth **[your mouth]** speaketh." Whatever your heart is full of, *that* is what will come out of your mouth.

7

Proverbs 18:21 teaches that "death and life is in the power of the tongue." Jesus said, in Mark 11:24c, "You will have what you say." This is because when you say something over and over again, what you say will eventually get down in your heart. So you have to be watchful of what you hear, see and say because these three are entrances into your heart. Once your heart is filled with what you have heard, seen and spoke you will have what you say.

I have been configured and engineered by God to allow His words of faith and power into my heart by absorbing His words through my eyes and my ears and speaking them out of my mouth. **THIS IS THE LAW OF RECEIVING**. Continuing this process will cause your heart to be so strong that even in the midst of challenging times, your heart will be greater than what you are facing.

Please remember, during our time together, the law of receiving is simply depositing the words of God into your heart through the process of hearing, seeing, and speaking the words of God!

Chapter 3

THE MAKE-UP OF THE HEART

In this chapter, I want to take a closer look at the word "heart" because of its importance in the receiving process. Proverbs 23:7 says, "As he thinketh in his heart, so is he: Eat and drink, saith he to thee; but his heart is not with thee." The English Standard Version (ESV) says, "For he is like one who is inwardly calculating. 'Eat and drink!' he says to you, but his heart is not with you." This verse is a very familiar verse, and so, many have read it without knowing the context or the setting. The setting is that of a selfish man urging you to eat and drink what he has set before you. He is giving you the impression that he wants you to enjoy everything, but in his heart, particularly his soul, he is THINKING something totally different.

Let me submit to you that the heart is the inner person, and it has two parts, namely, the human spirit and the soul. The soul consists of five components: mind, will, emotions, intellect, and imagination. But it is both the human spirit and soul that make up the heart of a person. **Heart, many times, is referred to as "the inner man" (Eph. 3:16; 2 Cor. 4:16; Rom. 7:22).**

Notice Matthew 9:4: "And Jesus knowing their thoughts said, Why are you **THINKING evil things in your HEARTS?**" Thinking is an activity of the mind, but the Lord Jesus asked the scribes why they were thinking in their hearts. **This shows that the MIND is part of the HEART**

Acts 11:23 says, "Who, when he arrived and saw the grace of God, rejoiced and encouraged them all to remain with the Lord with **PURPOSE of HEART**" (emphasis added). To "purpose" is to decide strongly to do something, which is an exercise of the will. **So, this verse shows that the WILL is part of the HEART (reference The New Strong Exhaustive Concordance of the Bible #4286).**

John 16:22 says, "Therefore you also now have sorrow, but I will see you again and **your HEART will REJOICE**, and no one takes your joy away from you" (emphasis added). Rejoicing is related to our emotions, but here, we see the heart rejoices, letting us know that **emotions are part of the HEART.**

In 1 Kings 3:9, Solomon says, "Give therefore thy servant an **UNDERSTANDING HEART** to judge the people, that I may discern between good and bad" (emphasis added). Understanding has to do with comprehending and digesting things mentally, which involves one's intellect. **So, this verse shows that INTELLECTUAL involvement is part of the HEART.**

Lastly, Genesis 6:5 says, "And God saw that the wickedness of man was great in the earth, and that every **IMAGINATION of the thoughts of the HEART** was only evil continually" (emphasis added). Imagination is about the ability of the mind to form images. **So, this verse shows that IMAGINATION is part of the HEART.**

Thus, it is extremely important to know that the heart of a person consists of the human spirit and the soul, and in particular, the mind. Your responsibility is to guard your heart because the purpose of your heart is to circulate and regulate life. The enemy wants to prevent life, but I declare that you will live life according to the purpose and plans of God!

Now that you have an understanding of the heart, notice how receiving the words of God is simply depositing words from God into your inner man, namely, your heart. Your heart is like soil, and whatever is planted in your heart will eventually appear and manifest in your life. I believe Proverbs 4:23 is worth repeating: "Keep thy HEART, human spirit and soul, with all diligence; for out of it are the issues of life" (emphasis added). When operating in the law of receiving, all you have to do is learn to plant the right seeds in your heart. When the right seeds are planted, then the right things will appear in your life.

If you are serious about changing your life's situations, conditions, and circumstances, make the correct deposits into your heart. If you are serious about the promises, plans, and purposes of God coming to pass in your life, prove it by making the right deposits into your heart.

For example, if you are believing God for healing to manifest in your life, PROVE IT. Go find healing scriptures (seeds) and deposit them into your heart. God's words contain His power and invaluable faith that can shape, mold, fashion, create, and configurate whatever you desire. The words of God are full of faith, and are exactly what you need in your heart.

Chapter 4

ACTING LIKE GOD

Any failure that you are experiencing in life is a failure to receive. In other words, if you are experiencing failure after failure in life, you as a believer have not deposited God's words properly in your heart If you fail to deposit the words of God into your inner man, you cannot make a withdrawal. It is impossible to release and speak faith-filled words if faith-filled words are not on the inside of you. Matthew 12:34b says, "For out of the abundance of the HEART the mouth speaks" (emphasis added). What this scripture is saying is that whatever the heart is full of, the mouth will speak it out! So, if I learn to deposit enough of God's words in my heart, I will begin to automatically speak what my heart is filled with. Proverbs 18:20 says, "A man's belly shall be satisfied with the fruit of his mouth; and with the increase of his lips shall be filled!" The Amplified Bible says it this way: "A man's stomach will be satisfied with the fruit of his mouth; He will be satisfied with the consequence of his words!" In other words, a man's experiences in life, along with his well-being, is totally connected to what comes out of his mouth. That's why it is vital to operate daily in the LAW OF RECEIVING.

My wife and I are now living and enjoying the receiving process, and it continues to allow us to live our best life with all of our needs being met. Praise God! You too can enjoy depositing and welcoming the words of God into your heart by seeing, hearing, and speaking

God's words! Once those words have filled your heart, you can speak and release them and have what you say!

The Bible says in Genesis 1:26a, "And God says let us make man in our image, after our likeness." Every born-again believer ought be acting like our Father God because we were made in His image and after His likeness.

When our Father God desired something, He spoke it. *God spoke what He desired.* However, the image of the thing He desired was already inside Him BEFORE He spoke it.

Pay attention now … When God spoke what He desired, what He desired came out of Him. Remember, what He desired was already in Him, but when He spoke it, it came out of Him.

Stay with me … What God desired came out of Him, carried by vehicles called words. Please note, these words were not just ordinary words; these words were filled with His faith and His creative power. When God released and spoke these words that were filled with His faith and power, Holy Spirit had already been moving, brooding, and hovering over the face of the waters. Why was Holy Spirit moving, brooding, and hovering? I will tell you why. Holy Spirit was waiting patiently on the words of faith from God our Father because faith is the substance needed to bring to pass what you are expecting!

When God released and spoke those faith-filled words, "Let there be light," He expected what He said and desired to be manifested because one of the responsibilities of Holy Spirit is to manifest the faith-filled words coming out of the heart and mouth of believers. Out of the abundance of the heart, the mouth speaks! Only Holy Spirit has the power to manifest faith-filled words.

This is why every believer should be enjoying the receiving process. We get to imitate God our Father. Hallelujah! I say we act like God our Father! Psalms 82:6 says, "I have said, Ye are gods; and all of you are children of the most High." It is time for every believer to act like God. But in order to release and speak words full of faith and power like our Father, we must deposit words full of faith and power!

St John 1:1 says, "In the beginning was the Word, and the Word was with God, and the Word was God."

St John 1:14 says, "And the Word was made flesh, and dwelt among us (and we beheld His glory as of the only begotten of the Father) full of grace and truth."

We know the Word is Jesus, the Son of God. When the Virgin Mary was told by the angel that she had found favor with God and that she would conceive a child, Mary asked a question in Luke 1:34: "Then said Mary unto the angel, How shall this be seeing I know not a man?"

Verse 35 says, "And the angel answered and said unto her, The Holy Ghost shall come upon thee and the power of the Holy Ghost shall over shadow thee."

Then later on, in verse 39, after the angel ministered to her more, Mary said, "Be it unto me according to thy word." She believed, received, and released words of faith. Glory to God! Right then, conception took place! I am telling you- Holy Spirit is waiting for faith-filled words to come out of your mouth so He can manifest them. **DEPOSIT, DEPOSIT, DEPOSIT** faith-filled words into your heart so you can speak them and Holy Spirit can have the necessary materials (faith-filled words) to deliver your desires! Whew!

Chapter 5

THERE IS WORK TO DO TO MAINTAIN A CLEAN HEART

I t is extremely important to the believer to know and understand we can imitate our Heavenly Father. As we deposit His words of faith into our heart and release them with our mouth, we can expect the God-kind of results, having exactly what we say.

It is also important to remember the heart has two parts, namely, our human spirit and our soul. In order to imitate our Father, we have to maintain a clean heart to manifest what we are believing.

Of course, once we are born again, our human spirit is changed, and it becomes alive to the things of God. But our soul (our mind, our will, our emotions, our intellect, and our imagination) has to be constantly maintained through the power of the Word of God. We have to work to maintain a clean heart to get the results we are believing.

James 1:21 says, "Wherefore lay apart all filthiness and superfluity of naughtiness, and receive with meekness the engrafted word which is able to save your souls."

The Amplified Bible's version says, "So get rid of all uncleanness and the rampant outgrowth of wickedness, and in a humble [gentle, modest] spirit receive and welcome the Word which implanted and rooted [in your hearts] contains the power to save your souls."

Years ago, when I read this scripture, I was somewhat confused because I received the Lord Jesus Christ as my personal Savior at the age of eight. I thought I was totally saved and did not need saving in any other areas of my life. My father, the (late) great Reverend A. J. Holmes Sr., was a powerful preacher and pastor. He baptized me and I thought that was all I needed. I was in church all of my life. I was a good Christian boy with good morals. I knew the scripture in Romans 10:9 that says, "That if thou shalt confess with thy mouth the Lord Jesus, and shalt believe in thine heart that God raised Him from the dead, thou shalt be saved."

Well, I did all of that. So what is James 1:21 really talking about? "Wherefore lay apart all filthiness and superfluity of naughtiness, and receive with meekness the engrafted word which is able to save your souls". Save my soul? My soul is already saved, is it not??

Before I answer this question, let me first establish that the Book of James was written to Christian believers and not unbelievers. So, it is not a mistake that James 1:21 is in our Bible.

Romans 5:12 (AMP) says, "Therefore, as sin came into the world through one man, and death as the result of sin, so death spread to all men, [no one being able to stop it or to escape its power] because all men sinned." Did you notice the scripture did not say "you" have sinned, but it said, "all" have sinned? Adam's sin and disobedience against God caused him to die spiritually. Physical death was passed upon ALL men.

Stay with me … Because of this, every person born into this world is spiritually dead and have no connection to God's kind of life, which consists of righteousness, peace, and joy in the Holy Ghost. Therefore, men, women, boys, and girls today have to be born again to be restored back to the position of right standing with God, as Adam was before he sinned and disobeyed God.

In the Gospel of St Luke 10:10 says, "For the Son of man is come to seek and to save that which was lost." It is imperative that we remember that Jesus came to planet earth to seek and to save the lost. Jesus died on the cross and was buried in a grave, but He rose from the dead on the third morning so that the world, through Him, might be "born again" and "saved." So, it is the will of God for all mankind to be saved. But in order for one to be saved (rescued and preserved from destruction), one must make a CHOICE to be in right standing before God. I have learned throughout my life that choices are extremely important. I have learned that life is choice-driven; you will live or die by the choices you make. You will succeed or fail based on the choices you make. I have also learned that the greatest choice you can make in life is receiving JESUS as your personal Lord and Savior!

St John 3:16 says, "For God so loved the world that He gave His only begotten Son, that whosoever believeth in Him should not perish, but have everlasting life."

God loves you, without a doubt, but that does not mean you are automatically saved or in right standing with Him. However, it *does* mean you have the opportunity to be saved, to be in right standing with Him. If you are not saved, or if you are not sure you are saved, pray this simple prayer right now:

> *Dear God, I know that without Jesus, I am lost. I believe Your Word that says if I confess with my mouth the Lord Jesus and believe in my heart that God raised Him from the dead, I shall be saved. I now invite You into my life and receive You by faith as my Lord and Savior. I am sorry for my sins, and I thank You for your for-giveness. Jesus, You are now my Lord. I am now born again, saved, a new creature in Christ, and a child of God. Thank You for saving me, in Jesus's name. Amen! PRAISE GOD!*

If you prayed that prayer for the first time, let me welcome you into the body of Christ!

Let us now discuss what really happens once you invite Jesus into your life. In order to understand this, one must first understand the makeup of man. 1 Thessalonians 5:23 says, "And the very peace of

God sanctify you wholly; and I pray God your whole **spirit soul** and **body** be preserved blameless unto the coming of our Lord Jesus Christ." This verse teaches us that we are tripartite beings in nature; we are spirit beings, possessing a soul and living in a physical body. Experiencing the new birth and becoming saved is a supernatural, spiritual matter. This supernatural, spiritual matter involves the Spirit of God transferring the new convert out of the kingdom of darkness and into the kingdom of God's dear Son.

Colossians 1:12-14 (AMP) says, "Giving thanks unto the Father, Who has qualified and made us fit to share the portion which is the inheritance of the saints [God's holy people] in the Light. [The Father] has delivered and drawn us to Himself out of the control and the dominion of darkness and has transferred us into the kingdom of the Son of His love, in Whom we have our redemption through His blood, [which means] the forgiveness of our sins."

WHAT POWERFUL SCRIPTURES WE HAVE IN THE WORD OF GOD!

Now, the question that has to be answered is, what happens when you become born again and saved? Well, the part of your heart called the human spirit, which had no connection with the Godly kind of life, is now made alive unto God and the things of God instantaneously! Born-again, or the new birth, simply deals with the **CONDITION** of the human spirit. The human spirit becomes alive to God and the Godly kinds of things.

Salvation, or being saved, deals with the **POSITION** you now have in life. The day you become born-again, God gives you the gift of salvation. Salvation is all about being positioned in life to have God's best. Salvation is not just limited to the born-again or new birth experience. Salvation is a very good gift from God our Father. Salvation positions us to be all that God created us to be. Salvation positions us to have all God planned for us to have. Salvation positions us to do all that God purposed us to do. What a wonderful gift from God, our Father.

Let's now answer what James 1:21 is really talking about. With all of the above writings in mind, let us read again James 1:21.

James 1:21 says, "Wherefore lay apart all filthiness and superfluity of naughtiness, and receive with meekness the engrafted word which is able to save your souls."

The Amplified Bible's version says, 'So get rid of all uncleanness and the rampant outgrowth of wickedness, and in a humble [gentle, modest] spirit receive and welcome the Word which implanted and rooted [in your hearts] contains the power to save your souls."

Let me give you a definition for "soul," which is the second part of your heart. **Soul can be defined as your mind, your will, your emotions, your intellect and your imagination**. (I want to thank my spiritual father, Apostle I. V. Hilliard, for teaching me this definition. I think it is the best definition for the soul). It is your soul that will govern how you think, feel and choose.

In answering what James 1:21 is talking about, believe me, everybody's soul need some work done to it. Here is why ... When you are born again, your soul does not change. Only your human spirit changes and becomes alive to God and the Godly kind of things. You still have old thought patterns that causes you to think in an ungodly manner. There is nothing that physically changes when you are born again. Your hands and feet do not look different. Your body is the same. You still think crazy thoughts, and your body wants to continue to do what is has been doing for all this time.

Now that your born-again human spirit is alive to God, you have the ability to overcome ungodly things. There is much work to be done on the soul. I now agree wholeheartedly with James 1:21, the soul need saving!

Remember, this book is entitled, *"ENJOYING THE RECEIVING PROCESS"*. There will be no enjoyment or receiving God's best if our soul is not changed. Once your soul is renewed and comes in agreement with your born-again human spirit, **ENJOYING THE RECEIVING PROCESS** will become part of your total makeup as a person, and you will begin to experience God's best over and over again. My wife and I are witnesses to how maintaining a clean heart (a born-again human spirit and soul) by depositing the Word of God in your life on a regular basis will position you for victory, success, and prosperity in every area of life. (More details on this supernatural experience in my upcoming book. Please, stay tuned.)

Chapter 6

BELIEVING AND RECEIVING GO TOGETHER

As a believer in the promises of God, it is of equal importance that you become a receiver of the promises of God. A believer should be a receiver. When I really had the revelation on this, it totally changed my life. I am a receiver of the promises of the words of God that I believe. My wife and I are constantly **believing AND receiving**! Working this process of believing and receiving over and over again causes you to live the best life while enjoying the process.

Jesus says in Mark 11:24, "Therefore I say unto you, what things soever you desire, when you pray, believe that you receive *them* [things], and you shall have *them [things] ...*"

The word "them" is italicized, and the italicized words were added by the translators. But let us remove the italicized words and gain a more powerful meaning: "Therefore I say unto you, what things soever you desire, when you pray, **believe** that you **receive** and you shall have" (emphasis added).

Believe that you **receive,** and you **shall have. BELIEVE, RECEIVE, HAVE.** You will only manifest in your life what you believed you received. Please get this: Believing *and* receiving the promises of God go together like wet and water. In actuality, if you *truly* believed, you have truly received, welcomed, and taken hold of the thing you believed. That is, if you really believed in the first place.

Biblical believing is all about accepting and receiving the words of God as being the truth, the absolute truth, nothing but the truth, and the "no doubt about it" truth. I may have no physical or natural evidence to prove what I have accepted as truth, but I trust God with all my heart. Biblical believing is really knowing. "Knowing what, Pastor?" Knowing God cannot lie to you. Even though my natural circumstance, situation, or condition may look the same, when I believe and receive, I *know* God cannot lie to me. You may not know exactly how it will come to pass, but because you trust God and His words, you know it will happen.

Numbers 23:19 says, "God is not a man that He should lie; neither the son of man that He should repent: Hath He said and shall He not do it? Or hath he spoken, and shall He not make it good?" Listen, if you have really believed and received (accepted) God's words as the truth (final authority in your life), then you know what you believed and received will manifest because God cannot lie to you. That which you believe **and** receive from God is absolute truth and nothing but the truth.

All of the believing and receiving takes place in the **heart** (Rom. 10:10a).

Heart represents your inner life or your inner man, namely, your spirit and your soul. **(Please refer back to Chapter 3: The Make Up of the Heart.)** You may not have any physical proof or evidence for what you believed you received, but your proof is that God said it, God promised it, and that is enough. **PRAISE GOD!**

Thank God for biblical believing, but biblical receiving is married to it. Biblical receiving is all about depositing that which you believed into your heart by working the law of receiving. Remember, the law of receiving is depositing the words of God into your heart through the process of hearing, seeing, and speaking the words of God. When you work this process over and over again, you will know God has granted that which you have believed and received, and it is just a matter of time before it appears! This is so exciting because you know you got it! You have this feeling of relief knowing that God's word is true and it is working on your behalf!!

Let us put Mark 11:24 all together now. Remember Mark 11:24 says "Therefore I say unto you, what things soever you desire, when you pray, believe that you receive them and you shall have them". What is Jesus saying? Jesus is saying, 1) believe and get to the state of knowing that what God says is truth, even though you may not have any physical proof or evidence; 2) believe that you have received or deposited those things which God said into your heart by hearing, seeing, and speaking them; 3) believe that out of your heart will come faith-filled words full of God's creative power, and 4) believe the Holy Spirit will take hold of your faith-filled words and cause them to manifest and then **you shall have**!

Start declaring, "I am a believer and a receiver." Believing and receiving go together.

Start doing yourself a favor and enjoy the receiving process.

Mark 9:23 says, "If thou canst believe, all things are possible, to him that believeth." Here, Jesus promises that if a person can believe (receive and accept God's Word as the truth without any physical evidence), that person can receive or deposit the promise of "all things becoming possible for them" in their heart. If a person continues to deposit what they believed and know is from God, that which they deposited will become possible for them.

Children of God began to accept what God says as "the truth" and deposit "the truth" in your heart and "the truth" will become possible for you. Everything God promised you is possible. Are you making the proper deposits? If you do your part, God has done His part. God cannot lie to you. He meant what He said and said what He meant. **God's words really work!**

I know it is the will of God for every believer to live their best life—a life that His Son, Jesus, paid the price for. God has so much for you. You may be experiencing some rough and difficult times right now, but it is not over. It is not going to end for you this way.

God has plenty more for you stored up. By faith, I know you can do this, so come on and join my wife and I and begin ENJOYING THE RECEIVING PROCESS!

Chapter 7

ENJOYING RECEIVING DURING CHALLENGING TIMES

M y wife, Lydecia, and I have not always been as successful
as we are currently. Our lives before we began *enjoying the
receiving process* were not lining up with the promises of God that we
had heard about in the Bible. We have been through a lot even though
we both were practically "born" in the church. My father, Reverend
A.J. Holmes, Sr., was a pastor for over fifty years. My wife's father, the
(late) great Reverend August Brown, was a pastor for over fifty years.
Pretty funny that my father and her father knew each other, and I knew
her father and she knew my father, but my wife and I did not know
each other. But one Friday evening, I, along with my brother and sister,
had to sing at her father's church. I entered the church, and I saw this
beautiful young woman playing the organ, and well, to make a long
story short, we started talking, and here we are thirty-eight years later,
married and glad about it!

My point in sharing a little of our background is simply to let you
know that although we were "raised" in church, serving and loving
the Lord, we were not living the abundant life that God planned for
us. Our lives *before* we began enjoying the receiving process was not
always a good witness to others. Now, do not misunderstand me, God
has always been good to us, and we have experienced blessings that
we knew only God could do. But frustration began to set in because we

would hear the promises of God in the Word of God, but these promises were not manifesting in our lives. Believe me, going to church *all* the time, serving in church, and spending more than what we were making became challenging in our marriage. We knew God had much better for us.

I never will forget, our very first year of marriage, we were contemplating divorce. Lydecia had secretly talked to a divorce attorney, and so did I. One night, we went to a church service, and an evangelist was preaching. In the middle of her message, she said, "It is a shame that two saved, tongue-talking people cannot get it together in marriage," and she went back to preaching her message. That statement hit both of us like a ton of bricks. It shook us! We were in church all the time, loving God, serving God, but not getting along, ready to divorce. We went home that night and had a long, serious talk, and we decided we would put forth much effort to be the couple in a marriage that pleased God.

So, we both started listening to the Word of God and focusing on our relationship to the point we started enjoying the process of receiving better for our marriage. We started communicating better, spending more quality time together, and laughing together. We made an agreement that we would let each other know if we did something that was not pleasing. There were times when I would say something that hurt her feelings and vice versa, and we would say something like, "That really was not nice. Is that what you really meant to say to me?" We did this over and over to the point where the things we use to argue about that caused us not to speak for days, we began to laugh about them, looking at each other and saying, "This does not make any sense."

We began to put forth an effort to do what the Word of God said about marriage. It caused our marriage to become much better, and we were *actually* enjoying the process. Of course, it did not happen overnight. This is not magic, nor did we take a "better marriage pill" and wake up in the morning and all was well. No, that was not the case, but a deposit here and a deposit there from the Word of God has caused

Lydecia and I to now have a very strong, healthy, satisfying, happy, awesome, amazing, stunning, and astonishing marriage! I think you get the picture. Enjoying the receiving process changed us from contemplating divorce to over thirty-eight years of marriage! IT WORKS! I will shout all by myself: HALLELUJAH!

First, we got our marriage together through *enjoying the receiving process*. We figured if it worked on our marriage, it could work on other things too. I remember the house we were living in. The mortgage company began foreclosure proceedings. This was devastating to us. We had to find another place to live for our family. Our credit was not good at all, and it was very challenging to get a loan for a new house. Many times, we would look at each other and laugh to keep from crying. There was not much *enjoying* going on at this time. But we stayed in the Word of God concerning the blessings of God over our lives. We would go over scriptures together and quiz each other on the memorization of certain scriptures. Enjoyment came back as we laughed when one of us did not say the scripture correct. Please understand, all we could depend on was the Word of God. So, "word time" was very important to us because this was time we were locking in *together* on the promises of God for our lives. We were getting in agreement with one another and with one accord. But as we quoted Scripture and made deposits, we knew we had grabbed hold of God's best for this situation. By faith, we knew God had granted us the desire of a place to reside in for our family. **WE KNEW IT**. We did not know how, but we knew it was done! Matthew 18:19 says, "Again I say unto you, That if two of you shall agree on earth as touching anything that they shall ask, it shall be done for them of my Father which is in heaven."

A few weeks before we had to move out of the foreclosed home, God raised up a person to help us. We were so highly favored to the point that we were able to move into a beautiful home in a great location with four bedrooms, three baths, a sprinkler system, and a three-car garage. Plus, we were renting with the option to buy! A happy wife meant a happy life for me. Things were really getting better for us. We were enjoying the receiving process.

Although things were going very well, three years later, we received some disturbing news from the owner of the house we were renting. The disturbing news was that her mortgage company had started a foreclosure proceeding on her months ago. As a matter of fact, we woke up one morning and saw the foreclosure sign. This was so upsetting because we were being forced to move out in just a few days. The short version of this story is that we submitted a bid for the house to purchase since we had been living there for the last three years. However, our bid was denied. We found out later that they did not want a pastor/preacher to have this type of house. So now, with just a few days to move, we were forced to move into a hotel. Again, not much *enjoying* going on at this time. Yes, my family was *homeless,* but we were able stay in a hotel for forty days and forty nights! The boys thought we were on vacation, enjoying life, because we did not complain. We stayed in the Word, kept quizzing one another on Scripture, and even had our boys preaching and teaching to us like we normally did in the home. I even made my famous chili in the hotel. The hotel manager did all she could to make our stay as comfortable as it could be. She would bake fresh oatmeal raisin cookies for me each afternoon at 4 p.m. My, my, my, oatmeal raisin cookies every day? Yes indeed, God is good.

Okay, back to the story … We knew God could not lie to us, so we kept on depositing, enjoying, and receiving the Word. During those forty days and forty nights, God raised up a man at a bank who helped us to get a mortgage for a brand-new house, and this man retired on the day he signed the papers. After forty days and forty nights of living in a hotel, on day forty-one we moved into a fully furnished home with five bedrooms, four baths, and a swimming pool! Tell me about God, and I will tell you about a Way Maker!

Let me also share with you the story of the repossession of our vehicle. We were so behind on our note that when I went to church, I had my deacons park really close to me in front and in the back so our car would not be towed. My wife and I would just laugh. But the repo man eventually got the vehicle, and here we go again.

We continued making deposits into our hearts concerning God's best for our lives. But during this repossession, we were more confident in the process than ever because we had witnessed it working in the past. Obviously, we were in dire need of a vehicle, and God raised up an owner of a used car dealership who worked out a deal for us based on the reference of one the members of the church. Say what you want, a used vehicle was much better than walking!

After a year, I was the owner a Ford Windstar. When I paid the final payment on the car two months later, the transmission went out completely. In order to repair the transmission, we needed a little over two thousand dollars—money we did not have. So, what do you think we did? We prayed. Yes, we prayed. We confessed. Yes, we confessed. We continued making deposits into our hearts. But you know what else we did? Let me tell you. We **drove** the vehicle. *Yes, we did.* It would start off really, really slow, but then, the acceleration would pick up. Other vehicles would be blowing their horns and looking at me, but I would just stay in my lane. Challenging times. But again, Lydecia and I would search the Word of God concerning financial prosperity and hear, see, and say those words and deposit them into our hearts. To give you the short version of this vehicle story, the Ford Windstar held up for four additional months, and by divine favor, we were able to buy a brand-new car and have been buying brand new vehicles ever since. Tell me about God, and I will tell you about a Savior!

Children of God, what I am telling you really works. If you can stay focused, because challenging times *will* come, you will manifest what you have deposited in your inner man. What really anchored Lydecia and I was the truth that God cannot lie to us. If God cannot lie to us, He must be telling the truth to us! Mark 13:31 says, "Heaven and earth shall pass away: but my words shall not pass away." His words will not pass away, but His words *will come to pass.* If His Word continues to come to pass in Lydecia and my life, His words will come to pass in your life. If you can stay focused while depositing the words of God, knowing He cannot lie to you, you too can begin enjoying the receiving process!

I know it is the will of God for every believer to live the best life that His Son, Jesus paid the price for. God has so much for you. You may be experiencing some rough and difficult times right now, but it is not over. It is not going to end for you this way. God's word is real. God's word is truth. Isaiah 55:11 says, "So shall my word be that goeth out of my mouth: it shall not return to me void, but it shall accomplish that which I please, and it shall prosper in the thing whereto I sent it". HALLEUJAH! God has plenty more for you stored up. God has proven His word to Lydecia and I over and over again. In the book of Acts 10:34 the scripture says, "Then Peter opened his mouth and said, Of a truth I perceive that God is no respecter of persons". By faith, I know you can do this. So come on and join my wife and I and begin **ENJOYING THE RECEIVING PROCESS!**

About the Author

Dr. Richard D. Holmes Sr. is the pastor of Morning View Word Church in Chicago, Illinois. His passion is to build competent viewers and doers of the Word of God and people of victory, success, and prosperity. The anointing that God has placed on his life causes him to teach in a very simple and understandable way. Dr. Holmes received his Doctorate in Ministry from G.M.O.R. Theological Seminary in 2003. He is married to Lydecia A. Holmes, who partners with him faithfully in ministry. Together, they have four sons: RaeDaeon, Richard Jr. (Shauta), DeAndre (Kassy), and Richaun. They have been blessed with six grandchildren: Reigh Grace, Avah, Richard III, Richaun II, DeAndre Jr., and Harmony.